For

Terri
_____

*with love
and deep appreciation

from*

Mother Myers
_____

_____ _Dec_ _____ 19 **77**

A Mother's Gifts

A Mother's Gifts

A Book of Praise and Inspiration

E. Jane Mall

Drawings by Billie Jean Osborne

Abingdon Press
Nashville, Tennessee

A Mother's Gifts

Library of Congress Cataloging in Publication Data

MALL, E. JANE, 1920-
    A mother's gifts.
    1. Mothers—Prayer-books and devotions—English.
I. Title.
BV283.M7M33   241'.6'43   75-33082

ISBN 0-687-27249-1

Scripture quotations noted RSV are from the Revised Standard Version of the Bible, copyrighted 1946, 1952, and 1971 by the Division of Christian Education, National Council of Churches, and are used by permission.

"For Faith in Loved Ones" and "Prayer on an Unwelcome Birthday" are from *Prayers for a Woman's Day* by Josephine Robertson. Copyright © 1957 by Abingdon Press.

Text on p. 24 is from *Plum Jelly and Stained Glass & Other Prayers* by Jo Carr and Imogene Sorley. Copyright © 1973 by Abingdon Press.

"The Prayer Perfect" is from *Joyful Poems for Children* by James Whitcomb Riley, copyright © 1941, 1946 and 1960 by Lesley Payne, Elizabeth Eitel Miesse and Edmund H. Eitel, reprinted by permission of the publisher, The Bobbs-Merrill Company, Inc.

"A Poet's Proverb" is from *A Poet's Proverb* by Arthur Guiterman © E. P. Dutton & Co., 1924. © renewed by Vida Lindo Guiterman.

Text on p. 16 is from "Selflessness" by David Edwards, *New Wine* Magazine, June, 1945, P.O. Box 22888, Fort Lauderdale, Fla. 33315. Reprinted with permission.

MANUFACTURED BY THE PARTHENON PRESS AT NASHVILLE, TENNESSEE, UNITED STATES OF AMERICA

*Dedicated to a mother who has
given me the precious gift of
love—my husband's mother,
Marie Elizabeth Mall.*

Foreword

In this book we celebrate motherhood, as well as the many and varied gifts which all women acknowledge and for which they are grateful.

As you read and reflect on the many gifts which you enjoy in your life, it is my sincere hope that you will make some exciting and perhaps even beneficial discoveries.

It may be that there is something in your life which you have not considered a particular blessing, and you will now see it in a different light. Perhaps you have received some gifts of which you have been totally unaware. There may be a gift you have not yet received and you wait for it now with anticipation.

These writings not only will help women understand and appreciate their gifts of life more fully, but also renew their stirrings of faith. To know that God is the author of all our gifts is to know true peace and contentment. The world gives us things and the world takes those things from us. Only those gifts which God bestows on us are lasting. At the same time, we are again made aware of the most perfect gift, Jesus Christ. If that were the only gift we ever received in a lifetime, it would be sufficient.

—*E. Jane Mall*

Contents

A Mother's Gifts

Two are better than one.
                    —*Ecclesiastes 4:9*

Love has many ways of expressing itself, but in general the ways are two—the practical and the sentimental. Which is the higher and better way? It is merely a question of appropriateness under the circumstances. Love must express itself very often in coal, and cornmeal, and salt pork, and clothes. But let it not be concluded that love may not express itself in acts of pure sentiment. The soul has needs. Sympathy and tenderness and friendship are just as real and more enduring, than coal and wood. Sometimes a flower is more important than flour; sometimes a word of cheer is better than gold.

—*Ferral*

Love is strong as death!

—*Song of Solomon 8:6*

Jesus said, "Ye are the salt of the earth." One of the first evidences about salt is the fact that it makes one thirsty. Does your marriage make others desire to take the same step? It should.

The two shall become one flesh.

—*Ephesians 5:31*

The Gift of Love and Marriage

Human love is another of the wonderful gifts of God. Men and women were made for one another. In Genesis we read that God said, "'It is not good that the man should be alone.'" We rejoice in this thing called love—it brings people together, it erases differences, it creates beauty. "Behold, you are beautiful, my beloved, truly lovely" (Song of Sol. 1:16).

Of course, life is not always lovely and bright and shiny. Every wife knows that. There are times when life is sad or tragic or hard. There are times when life is just plain dull and boring. We know how difficult it would be to live through these times without becoming disheartened if it weren't for the fact that we can share them with the one we love. Shared burdens are lighter, and we thank God for the gift of human love.

The love shared between a man and a woman is beautiful. We see them in their youth, with starry eyes, promising to love each other forever. Through the years they experience many things together—some happy and good, some sad and discouraging. Together they are able to weather storms and to accept the good times as gifts from a loving God. In their old age they still sustain each other and give comfort and care and a sense of belonging and worth to each other that no one else can give. A good, solid marriage, rooted in a deep faith in God, nourished by his presence and sustained by his love, is one of the most beautiful facts of life.

Christian mothers know that even the very ability to love comes from God and they are grateful to him for this precious gift. Because it's from God they nurture it with soft words of love and acceptance. They stand by their husband's side, co-workers and lovers together. They weather the storms of life and the tragedies and the hard times, knowing that what would be impossible to bear alone, they will survive because they're together.

They are also aware of the fact that in their real love for each other, a husband and wife are giving a special gift to their children. They are silently telling their children about the goodness and stability and enduring qualities of human love. And they show too that it is very like the love which God has for all of us.

Dear Lord, I am so thankful for a loving husband. His love, his protection, his concern for me, are so dear. Please, dear God, keep special watch over him. We need him so much! Amen.

And you shall teach them to your children, talking of them when you are sitting in your house.
—Deuteronomy 11:19 RSV

He is happiest, be he king or peasant, who finds peace in his home

—*Goethe*

A house is built of logs and stone,
  Of tiles and posts and piers;
A home is built of loving deeds
  That stand a thousand years.
                    —*Victor Hugo*
                      "House and Home"

Is your place a small place?
  Tend it with care;—
    He set you there.

Is your place a large place?
  Guard it with care!—
    He set you there.

Whate'er your place, it is
  Not yours alone, but His
    Who set you there.
                    —*John Oxenham*
                      "Your Place"

The Gift of Home

We may live in a large house, in an apartment, or in a trailer. The place we call home may be lavish with expensive furnishings, or it may be quite humble. Whatever it's like, it's home for us, and it's where our families live and grow.

All mothers are aware of the importance of home life. Each mother, in her own distinctive way, makes of the place in which she lives a home for her family.

She strives for comfort and cleanliness and beauty. Her home is a place which is unlike any other, the place all members of her family regard as their home. All mothers know of the importance of home, and all mothers hope for a home life their children will cherish with happy memories.

The Christian mother has an added responsibility which she gladly shoulders—that of making Christ the head of their home. She knows that it is there, in the home, where her children will learn of Christ and his love. She will expose her children to the teachings of the church, but she knows that it is in the home where they will discover whether or not it's all true.

A home where there is no real love or affection, no true peace of mind, no comfort for the soul, is not a home that speaks of the love of Christ. So the Christian mother stays close to God—her source of strength and knowledge—and she knows how to make any dwelling a Christian home for her family.

We know all too well that the world holds many dangers and pitfalls. We watch as, one by one, our children leave the warm safety of home, and we fear for them. We wish that we could go with them and protect them, but that's not possible or desirable.

The Christian mother can be comforted and feel secure in the knowledge that, because her children grew up in a Christian home, they are well fortified against the dangers and temptations that wait for them. In the Christian home, all problems and questions are solved through prayer, through leaning on the mercy and the goodness of God. All celebrations are a matter of thanksgiving to him who gives us all our blessings. From this kind of home emerge men and women who possess a strength of character and a love for all of God's creation which nothing or no one will ever destroy.

The gift of a Christian home is one of our most precious gifts. God's presence, with all its strength and solace and joy, adds another dimension to the word *home*.

Lord, my home is no castle! It's not always clean and shiny and the furniture is getting shabby. But it's home, and we love being there together. Without your presence, it wouldn't be a home of love, a place to be at peace within its walls. We need you always, dear Lord, to make where we live a real home.   Amen.

*Lo, children are an heritage of the Lord:
and the fruit of the womb is his reward.*
—Psalm 127:3

Thank you, God,

for little humdrum jobs like peeling apples and washing dishes.

They give me a *chance* to communicate with my children.

There's something about having my hands busy that frees my mind—that permits my thinking to rise above the humdrum tasks. And there's something about being involved in a common task that unites us. . . .

"Remember the time when . . . ?"
"What do you think about . . . ?"
"I used to feel that way, too."
"Have you read . . . ?"
"The other day my teacher said . . . "
"I wonder . . . "

Our minds wander along together while our hands are busy with the task.

Thank you, Father, for such humdrum tasks . . . and for these who do them with me.   Amen.

Dear Father, may my faith in those I love never falter. When they are away or when they seem to do things I cannot understand, give me the faith to remember the fine qualities which have always made me so proud and the understanding to realize that in every life there are some factors another cannot know. Help me always to trust and not judge, to the end that when the situation is clear, I may truly say that my confidence never faltered.   Amen.

—*Josephine Robertson*
"For Faith in Loved Ones"

24

The Gift of Family

Among the many gifts God has given us, one of the greatest is our family. We are one unit made up of a number of people. Sometimes we're happy together, sometimes we quarrel; sometimes we help one another, sometimes we hurt; sometimes we are a source of strength to one another and sometimes we lean too heavily for support. But by the grace of God, it is our family and we're glued together by our mutual love, and we thank God for this precious gift.

And yet, how do we treat this gift? Do we come near to destroying it with petty feelings and selfishness and greed and impatience and thoughtless acts? Little things that aren't much in themselves, perhaps, but put together may destroy us? "'Catch us the foxes'" Scripture says, "'the little foxes, / that spoil the vineyards, / for our vineyards are in blossom'" (Song of Sol. 2:15 RSV).

Families are of all kinds: poor, wealthy, happy, fighting, loyal, divided. The descriptions are endless. How family members relate and respond to one another tells what kind of a family they are. We Christian mothers are concerned about our families. We want them to show the qualities that Christ would have them show. What can we do to keep peace and harmony and love and forgiveness and patient understanding and kindness in our family?

We can read the story of Ruth. Her family life was in terrible shape. It would have been easy to give up, to leave it behind, and try for a new life for herself. But Ruth didn't succumb to this temptation. Her love was strong and enduring, and we can follow her example.

Hannah prayed and prayed and never gave up. Women like this have changed the world. We can believe in the power of prayer to change things and never stop praying.

Abigail was a wise woman and acted as mediator. How often we mothers are called upon to act as mediators in our families! We can't take sides, so in order to keep peace, we are the mediators.

As Christian mothers we need to think of ourselves as channels of love and Christ's peace. We fill ourselves daily with his word; we go to him in prayer, we are assured of his help. There will be times when we will find it difficult to be happy or to forgive or to be patient—but we'll be content knowing that God can do, through us, what we can't do ourselves.

We want love within our family circle and peace, and we daily strive for this. Blessed be the Christian mother who holds her family together with this kind of love!

Dear God, you know how very much I love my family, how much I want them to be happy and fulfilled. Help me to curb my impatience, to show more of my love, to put a leash on my temper. They love me and they need me, and I want to be worthy of them. Without you I can't do it, God. Amen.

Can two walk together,
except they be agreed?

—Amos 3:3

*'Tis the human touch in this world that
      counts,
  The touch of your hand and mine,
  Which means far more to the fainting heart
    Than shelter and bread and wine;
  For shelter is gone when the night is o'er,
    And bread lasts only a day,
  But the touch of the hand and the sound of
      the voice
    Sing on in the soul alway.*
                    —Spencer Michael Free
                    "The Human Touch"

A blessed thing it is for any man or woman to have a friend: one human soul whom we can trust utterly: who knows the best and the worst of us, and who loves us in spite of all our faults; who will speak the honest truth to us, while the world flatters us to our face, and laughs at us behind our back; who will give us counsel and reproof in the day of prosperity and self-conceit; but who, again, will comfort and encourage us in the day of difficulty and sorrow, when the world leaves us alone to fight our own battle as we can.

                              —Kingsley

Two are better than one; because they have a good reward for their labour. For if they fall, the one will lift up his fellow.

                    —Ecclesiastes 4:9-10

The Gift of Friendship

All of us need friends. We need someone to talk to and to listen to. Someone to confide in, someone who will share our burdens and our joys. We need a person who loves us in spite of our faults and who understands us. Life without a friend is cold and lonely.

So we reach out to others, hoping to meet that person who will become our friend. When we were children we came home with a smile and said, "I've found a friend!" As teen-agers we confided in our friends and told them things we wouldn't have revealed to anyone else. Women rely very much on their special friends. More problems are solved and hurts healed over a cup of coffee between friends than will ever be known. Men too have their golfing buddies and tennis partners. We need our friends, and we feel pity for a person who goes through life without a special friend.

Over a lifetime we may have many friends. We move into a new neighborhood and, out of the many people we meet, one becomes a special friend. Nothing dramatic, just a helping hand when needed, a realization that you talk the same language concerning so many things, a laugh or a smile that says, "I want to be your friend," and it grows day by day. The gift of friends is another of the God-given gifts we enjoy.

We know that in order to have a friend we must be a friend, and so we reach out and give a helping hand, offer a cup of coffee, look for ways to help another person and—Serendipity! we find a friend.

It's difficult to imagine what life would be like without our friends. They give an added dimension to our lives. We are content to spend hours with husband and children because they are the core of our lives; but we need something else, something a friend brings to us in a special way. Shared confidences lessen burdens and shared work is more than twice as easy. Sometimes a certain happiness bubbles up inside us, and it's made even better through the sharing of it with a friend.

We thank God for this precious gift of friendship that shows us what true unselfishness is, what a sharing of love and concern for one another can be. It's another gift from God we cherish.

Dear God, I am so grateful for my friends. There are times when I don't want to talk to my children or to my husband, and I'm thankful I have a friend I can run to. When I'm blue, she cheers me up; when I'm happy, she shares my joy; when I'm lonely, she's there. I don't know what my life would be like without a friend, Lord, and I hope I never will! Bless my friends, and help me to always be a friend.   Amen.

Ye call upon me, and ye shall go and
pray unto me, and I will hearken unto you.
—*Jeremiah* 29:12

Pray without ceasing.

–I Thessalonians 5:17

The Lord's Prayer contains the sum total of religion and morals.

—Wellington

Dear Lord! Kind Lord!
  Gracious Lord! I pray
Thou wilt look on all I love,
  Tenderly today!
Weed their hearts of weariness;
  Scatter every care
Down a wake of angel-wings
  Winnowing the air.

Bring unto the sorrowing
  All release from pain;
Let the lips of laughter
  Overflow again;
And with all the needy
  O divide, I pray,
This vast measure of content
  That is mine today!
        —James Whitcomb Riley
        "The Prayer Perfect"

All things, whatsoever ye shall ask in prayer, believing, ye shall receive.

—Matthew 21:22

The Gift of Prayer

We've all known days when there were too many things to do all at once—the ironing piled high, dishes stacked in the sink, and the beds unmade. The phone rings, something on the stove boils over, and one of the children clings to your knees, crying for a kiss of comfort.

What does a mother do? She puts first things first! She ignores the ironing and the dishes and the unmade beds. She turns off the stove and takes her sobbing child in her arms, sits down, and holds him close to her heart. He snuggles close to her and closes his eyes. It's quiet time, a tiny island of peace in the hectic day. Perhaps it's a moment for prayer.

The Christian mother knows the value and the importance of prayer. We read "Pray without ceasing" (I Thess. 5:17), and it sounds beautiful, but we wonder how we can pray without ceasing when there are days on end when we never find time to even once drop to our knees. It's impossible to pray without ceasing! Our prayer times, although precious, are all too seldom. To be alone with God, in loving conversation with him, are the times we look forward to, but there is so little time!

Of course, this kind of prayer is not always possible, but we can live in a spirit of prayer all the time. While we're washing those dishes or ironing, we can talk with God. We can turn off the TV and the radio and, in the stillness, communicate with him. When we drive to the supermarket our thoughts can be of him. That's prayer!

33

There's another way to pray without ceasing. In the myriad of decisions to be made each day, we can ask God to help us do the right thing, to make the correct judgment, to decide the correct action to take. That's prayer!

When our children complain that something is going wrong or not working out the way they hoped, we can suggest that they take it to God. And we can let them know that we will be praying for them. In our daily conversations we can be talking to God. That's prayer!

Once we get into the habit of feeling his presence at all times, we'll realize that to pray without ceasing isn't impossible after all. Little by little, prayer will become a constant in our lives and our days will be easier for it.

With all of God's gifts we have the option to ignore them or to gratefully receive them and make them a living, vital part of ourselves. Surely, the gift of prayer is one the Christian mother accepts with thanksgiving.

Oh, Lord, dear Lord, it would be wonderful if I could have more time for prayer. But you know that I never do! There are so many jobs to do and people to talk to—so much on my mind! Help me see that there are more little islands of quiet than I know, and help me use them to talk more often with you. Amen.

34

We are labourers together with God.
—I Corinthians 3:9

Whatsoever ye do in word or deed, do all in the name
of the Lord Jesus.

—*Colossians 3:17*

My heart rejoiced in all my labour: and this was my
portion of all my labour.

—*Ecclesiastes 2:10*

I was too ambitious in my deed,
and thought to distance all men in success,
Till God came on me, marked the place, and
*   said,*
"Ill-doer, henceforth keep within this line,
Attempting less than others"—and I stand
And work among Christ's little ones, content.
*   —Elizabeth Barrett Browning*
*   "Content"*

God's Road is all uphill,
*   But do not tire,*
Rejoice that we may still
*   Keep climbing higher.*
*   —Arthur Guiterman*
*   "A Poet's Proverb"*

The Gift of Work

What part does God have in the eight or more hours of each day in which we work? We clean house or sit at a desk or run a machine or wait on customers. Some of us work all day at a job and come home to a few more hours of work. What does God have to do with these hours?

We may say, "Well, God doesn't have much to do with that; that's work." We go to church and read our Bibles and we pray. Certainly he's present at these times. He's also there when we hold our child or listen to a friend or spend quiet time with our husbands. But when we work? Maybe, in a way, because we love him, but it's difficult to see him as a real, living part of our work.

Martin Luther said that God's attitude toward repentant sinners is like that of a loving mother toward a child imperfectly toilet trained. He cleanses us from our sins as a mother changes diapers. The kind of love we believe in doesn't shrink from the most disagreeable tasks.

We can't put Christ into some religious niche of our hearts and lives and say, "He belongs here—with my Bible and my prayer life" and "He doesn't belong here where life is sometimes pretty grubby."

One of the most important things we can do as Christians is to make God such an all-invading part of our lives that everyone will see that he makes a vital difference in our family and our work. We don't have to work all the time, and we're grateful for that. Sometimes we say, "I've got some time to kill." If we think about it, time is a precious gift from God, and it is not something to be wasted apart from him. Perhaps we'll use an extra hour here and there relaxing, resting, not even thinking about anything in particular. But in a God-directed, God-filled life, even that is good and he can be a part of it. In a sense, even these so-called idle moments can be a working time for us.

We can begin to scrub a dirty floor or to type a dull business report or listen to an impatient customer or to change a diaper or just to relax and say to ourselves, "God, I know that in your eyes all honest work is honorable and can be done to your glory. Help me to see this more clearly!

And then, praise God, we will realize that we have yet another gift for which to be thankful—the gift of honest labor, done to his glory.

Well, God, as you know, I do complain sometimes about work. I get tired of washing dishes every day and doing the laundry every week and scrubbing the same floors over and over. My family just makes the dishes and the clothes dirty again and they track mud on the floors. Still, even the dirtiest, messiest job can be done to your glory, if I see it that way. Will you help me with this? Amen.

He hath made every thing beautiful in his time.
—Ecclesiastes 3:11

Beauty does not lie in the face. It lies in the harmony between man and his industry. Beauty is expression. When I paint a mother I try to render her beautiful by the mere look she gives her child.

—*Jean Francois Millet*

Whatsoever things are lovely, . . . think on these things.

—*Philippians 4:8*

> *There is beauty in the forest*
> *When the trees are green and fair,*
> *There is beauty in the meadow*
> *When wild flowers scent the air.*
> *There is beauty in the sunlight*
> *And the soft blue beams above.*
> *Oh, the world is full of beauty*
> *When the heart is full of love.*
> —*Author unknown*
> *"When the Heart Is Full*
> *of Love"*

Beauty hath so many charms one knows not how to speak against it; And when a graceful figure is the habitation of a virtuous soul—When the beauty of the face speaks out the modesty and humility of the mind, it raises our thoughts up to the great Creator; but after all, beauty, like truth, is never so glorious as when it goes the plainest.

—*Sterne*

The Gift of Beauty

What is beauty? Where does it come from? We look at a picture of someone we know and we say, "Oh, she's much prettier than that!" Or we see someone's portrait and we say, "The artist didn't capture her real beauty."

A man says, "Irene is the most beautiful person I know." Someone else says, "What does he see in Irene? She's not even pretty!" Beauty is, after all, in the eye of the beholder.

Aristotle called beauty "the gift of God." Certainly, God has created all of us with potential beauty. Through obedience to him we truly become beautiful. "I beseech you therefore, brethren, by the mercies of God that ye present your bodies a living sacrifice, holy, acceptable unto God" (Rom. 12:1). If we will let him have his way in our lives we will be happy and we will be holy and acceptable unto him. And if we're acceptable to him, we're beautiful!

This kind of obedience adds beauty to a person's whole being. There is power under the surface that shines through and attracts others.

I feel very sorry for the women who spend so much money on creams and lotions and makeup and weekly visits to the hairdresser and neglect the most important ingredient of beauty. Because the day is going to come when all the cream and makeup and beauty salons won't be able to help. And then a person must face what has been inside all the years of her life.

We've all heard young people talk about their

beautiful mothers. Then we see that mother and we think, "Why, she's not beautiful at all! Her nose is too large (or too small) and she's overweight (or underweight). She's not a beautiful woman at all!"

It's all right to use creams and lotions and makeup and go to the beauty parlor to have our hair washed and set. Certainly it's all right to keep ourselves neat and clean. However, the first thing for us to think about is our obedience to God and his will for our lives. We must try daily to be more like him, to become holy and acceptable to God. Then the beauty within, from Christ, will shine through.

The way we act, the decisions we make, the love we show—all these things result from the laws that are "written on our hearts." From this comes beauty of a very special nature.

Oh, dear God, I look in the mirror and I know that I'm not beautiful. There are so many things wrong with me! Still I do know that beauty fades eventually, that no one keeps it forever. Help me to acquire the beauty from within that comes from you and will never go away. Amen.

*The grass withereth, the flower fadeth: but
the word of our God shall stand for ever.*
—Isaiah 40:8

The study of God's Word, for the purpose of discovering God's will, is the secret discipline which has formed the greatest characters.

—*J. W. Alexander*

Lay up his words in thine heart.

—*Job 22:22*

> *Within this ample volume lies*
> *The mystery of mysteries.*
> *Happiest they of human race*
> *To whom their God has given grace*
> *To read, to fear, to hope, to pray,*
> *To lift the latch, to force the way;*
> *But better had they ne'er been born*
> *That read to doubt or read to scorn.*
> —*Sir Walter Scott*
> *"The Book of Books"*

The Scriptures teach us the best way of living, the noblest way of suffering, and the most comfortable way of dying.

—*Flavel*

In the beginning was the Word, and the Word was with God, and the Word was God.

—*John 1:1*

The Bible is a window in this prison of hope, through which we look into eternity.

—*Dwight*

The Gift of Scripture

I lost my glasses and spent more than half an hour looking for them. Finally, I was able to sit down and read the newspaper—after I located my glasses pushed up over my own forehead!

Ever have anything like that happen to you? The time I wasted! How foolish I felt! I needed them so much, and they were right there all the time.

As we go through life we meet many situations: a child is ill; Dad gets a raise and some decisions must be made; a relative dies and the children demand an explanation. Life goes on, and we want most to be able to handle all of it. We need to know how to handle the good times as well as the bad.

How can we know the right things to do in all our circumstances? When something happens—good or bad—is it possible for us to have the right knowledge stored in our hearts and minds for instant use?

It's like the glasses that weren't really lost. We have our Bibles ready and waiting to fill us with knowledge, with the truth of God's will for our lives, with wisdom and the power of the Holy Spirit. Through the daily reading and studying of his precious word, we fill our very being with strength for the times to come.

Many of our days go smoothly, without incident, and we're grateful for those islands of peace. In the midst of them, we open our Bibles and search God's word for meaning for our lives and the lives of our loved ones. We ask him for insight to know and understand his will. We pray for the wisdom to rightfully handle future happenings. We bask in his word and let it fill our hearts and minds, confident that it is stored somewhere deep inside us, ready for the time when we will need it.

The person who has relied heavily, daily on the reading and study of his word will surely still ask for help, but she will have something else: a storehouse within that lessens the gap between herself and her God. As she draws from this storehouse she will find the right words to say, the comforting sounds to make, the help she needs in decision-making.

The Bible lies on tables in many homes. In some it is something to be dusted and displayed; in some it is put away and never used. The Christian woman is aware of her continuing need to read her Bible, and she's also aware of this part of her influence on her family. In later years, when her children think about and talk about Mother, they will remember the Bible held in her hands, used daily, and they will want to go there for the same wisdom and strength.

Lord, your word is so precious to me! When I'm starting down the wrong path, it shows me the better way. When I'm discouraged, it lifts my spirit. When I feel weak and inept, it gives me strength, and when I'm afraid it gives me courage. I cannot be a good mother without your word to guide me, dear Lord, so please don't let me ever neglect it.   Amen.

My soul shall be joyful in the Lord:
it shall rejoice in his salvation.

—Psalm 35:9

These things have I spoken unto you, that my joy might remain in you, and that your joy might be full.

—*John 15:11*

Lord God, how full our cup of happiness!
We drink and drink—and yet it grows not less;
But every morn the newly risen sun
Finds it replenished, sparkling, over-run!
Hast Thou not given us raiment, warmth, and meat,
And in due season all earth's fruits to eat?—
Work for our hands and rainbows for our eyes,
And for our souls the wings of butterflies?—
A father's smile, a mother's fond embrace,
The tender light upon a lover's face?—
The talk of friends, the twinkling eye of mirth,
The whispering silence of the good green earth?—
Hope for our youth, and memories for age,
And psalms upon the heavens' moving page?

And dost Thou not of pain a mingling pour,
To make the cup but overflow the more?
                    —*Gilbert Thomas*
                    "The Cup of Happiness"

Happiness is like manna; it is to be gathered in grains, and enjoyed every day. It will not keep; it cannot be accumulated; nor have we got to go out of ourselves or into remote places to gather it, since it is rained down from Heaven, at our very doors.

—*Tryon Edwards*

48

The Gift of Joy

Joy—celebrate—fun—smile—laugh. These are happy words that make us think of good times and friends and special days in our lives. They are words that describe our celebration of life, in all its various aspects, and we like to think about them and remember.

It would be wonderful to be happy all the time, but we know that's not possible. Still, we know people who seem to be happy most of the time. People who face life with a positive, happy attitude; and then we know others who are negative and frowning a good bit of the time. What makes the difference? Is there some special secret we should know about? Of course there is! Jesus gave us the secret word when he summarized the law: Love. He said to love God and neighbor and from that will stem our joy in life.

Of course, going around with a grin all the time isn't happiness. Our joy must come from a deeper place within ourselves. We very seldom feel joy or happiness alone. We usually don't smile or laugh or celebrate all by ourselves. And we can't really celebrate life all alone—we need others to share the joy with us. If we have a genuine love for others we will make their joy our joy.

We belong to God and we belong to one another and therein lies our joy. We can curse the darkness, concentrate on the negative, face life with a frown if we want to. Or we can light candles, be positive, and show the joy which is in our hearts. It's our choice, and that choice determines our happiness.

The Christian mother knows the difference between a quarreling, negative, unhappy family and one which is happy and delighted with one another and with life. We all strive for peace and happiness in our families. Perhaps we can convince one another that because of God's love for us and our love for one another we can be a happy, contented family. Peace and contentment within our family won't come to us unbidden. We have to work at it. We have to appreciate anew, over and over, the great gift God has given us in the gift of others to share our joy and to realize how empty life would be without others to love and be loved by.

If we truly believe that our lives are run according to God's will for us and that he loves us very much and that he has great and wonderful things in store for us and that we have received the gift of one another from his generous hand, how can we be anything *but* filled with joy?

Oh, God, I'm glad that we don't have to be serious and somber all the time! Because I take such joy in the laughter of my children, in the smile of my husband, in a sunset, and in a sparkling, clean rain. So many things! When my lemon meringue pie is perfection or when my husband calls me beautiful, I am so happy. Just little things, Lord, but they bring a large measure of happiness and joy to my life, and I'm grateful for them. Amen.

There shall be no more death,
neither sorrow, nor crying,
neither shall there be any more pain.
　　　　　—Revelations 21:4

I reckon that the sufferings of this present time are not worthy to be compared with the glory which shall be revealed in us.

—*Romans 8:18*

Sorrow is our John the Baptist, clad in grim garments, with rough arms, a son of the wilderness, baptizing us with bitter tears, preaching repentance; and behind him comes the gracious, affectionate, healing Lord, speaking peace and joy to the soul.

—*Huntington*

Tears are the safety valve of the heart
When too much pressure is laid on it.
—*Albert Smith*

Christ also suffered for us, leaving us an example, that ye should follow his steps.

—*I Peter 2:21*

Keep me from bitterness. It is so easy
To nurse sharp bitter thoughts each dull dark
  hour.
Against self-pity, Man of sorrows, defend me,
With Thy deep sweetness and Thy gentle
  power.
And out of all this hurt of pain and
  heartbreak
Help me to harvest a new sympathy
For suffering human kind, a wiser pity
For those who lift a heavier cross with Thee.
  —*Violet Alleyn Storey*
  "*Prayer in Affliction*"

The Gift of Trials

If God is so good and loves us so much, why is there suffering and pain and tragedy? It's a question we can't help but ask.

There was a young pastor and his wife dedicated to the church, spending their days working for Jesus Christ. All their energies were directed toward showing their love for Christ. Their teen-aged son, riding his bicycle, was hit by a motorist and killed. Why did this happen?

Rizpah, in the Old Testament, saw her two sons killed. No one would even give them a decent burial! Why this kind of suffering?

We all know of so many stories like this. We believe in a loving, compassionate God, so why do these tragedies happen? Could there be any reason or sense to them at all?

God wants only the best for his own, and he doesn't cause these things to happen. He simply chooses not to intervene. But his hopes are for us—that we will be strong enough to allow him to use these things for our good. If we're open and yielding to him and his will, he will enter our hearts and give us strength and courage—more than we thought possible. We will mature in our faith.

The pastor and his wife whose son was killed organized the Society of Compassionate Friends, and whenever anyone suffers a loss similar to theirs they offer comfort and understanding and help on the way to the healing of the spirit. This group has grown to a large number of people who spend a lot of time forgetting self and loving others. There is no room in their hearts for bitterness. With God's help they are growing as Christians.

Rizpah sat for five months watching over the bodies of her two sons. She sat through scorching sun and pouring rain and cold nights, keeping birds and animals away from her loved ones. She was determined that her sons should have a decent burial, so she sat there, protecting them, until her prayers were answered. Her strength to do this came from God.

It's difficult to imagine going through something like this. (We wonder how we'd bear up under such tragedy.) We know that some turn tragedy into a victory of sorts and others are crushed and withdraw from life.

What makes the difference? We must ask ourselves where our security lies. In a person, a career, a condition of life, or solely in God? If God comes first in our lives, and we trust in him alone for our security, we too will be able to turn the tragedies of life into victory. He stands ready and waiting to help us to do this. Then we can thank him for another gift—strength through trials.

Oh, God, there was a time when I couldn't have given you thanks for a trial in my life! But I see now that out of the trials in my life I have gained strength. So, dear Lord, even though I know that you don't send those trials, I do know that you will always use them for good in my life. Thank you for that. Amen.

God is not the author of confusion,
but of peace.
—I Corinthians 14:33

Oh, the little birds sang east,
  and the little birds sang west,
And I smiled to think God's greatness
  flowed around our incompleteness,—
Round our restlessness, his rest.
        —Elizabeth Barrett Browning
        "Round Our Restlessness"

All thy children shall be taught of the Lord; and great
shall be the peace of thy children.
                                    —Isaiah 54:13

With eager heart and will on fire,
I strove to win my great desire.
"Peace shall be mine," I said; but life
Grew bitter in the barren strife.

My soul was weary, and my pride
was wounded deep; to Heaven I cried,
"God grant me peace or I must die;"
The dumb stars glittered no reply.

Broken at last, I bowed my head,
Forgetting all myself, and said,
"Whatever comes, His will be done;"
And in that moment peace was won.

                        —Henry van Dyke
                        "Peace"

The Crown of the House is Godliness
The Beauty of the House is Order
The Glory of the House is Hospitality
The Blessing of the House is Contentment.
                        —Old inscription

The Gift of Contentment

Contentment. What does that word mean? Does it mean being happy with our lot in life? Taking what comes without complaint and making the best of it? Does it mean never feeling dissatisfaction or unrest? Does it mean being satisfied?

As the farmer said, "Only pigs is satisfied."

Contentment is not a passive emotion, something that comes to us and that we accept and allow to become a part of us. It's not a wishy-washy emotion, either. It is most certainly not a matter of being placid and not caring about anything.

True contentment is hard won. For the Christian mother it's a matter of relying on God for all things, of having absolute trust in his wisdom and his goodness and his love. There will be trials and unhappiness and storms in our lives. All days will not be peaceful days. Children will become ill, money will be short, plans will be upset, friends will disappoint us, and there will be tears. The woman who has built within herself the sure knowledge that God is still running things in his world will experience a deep feeling of contentment.

Some try Yoga and going into a trance or reading the writings of ancient philosophers to achieve contentment. Some believe that contentment comes from being smarter than anyone else or wealthier or more beautiful. Some put their trust in possessions. However, we know that these things do not, in themselves, bring true contentment.

The Christian mother knows that it is through the

reading and study of God's Word, through daily prayer, through a feeling of oneness with God, that the certainty of his loving presence becomes clearer and more and more convincing. With this truth comes contentment.

The Christian mother says, "I know that all things work together for good to those who love God," and she is aware that that means *all* things. The unhappy events of life, the tragedies, the frustrations, everything that happens can work together for positive good in the life of a Christian. Knowing this, the Christian mother feels contented.

We still fight the frustrations, cry over disappointments, and cope the best we can with the tragedies and hurts that storm into our lives. Of course! The difference is that deep inside, where it counts, we are serene. We have put our lives into God's hands and he's in charge. Nothing that happens will ever cause him to be discouraged or frustrated. He will never give up and let us go.

Being sure of this, feeling his great love for us, is our source of true contentment. It's a gift which is ours for the taking.

Dear Lord, without you I'd be so restless and unsure and afraid. It's only because I know that you love me and that you're in control of my life that I can feel contented. Help me to impart this feeling of contentment to my children, too. And stay with me, God.   Amen.

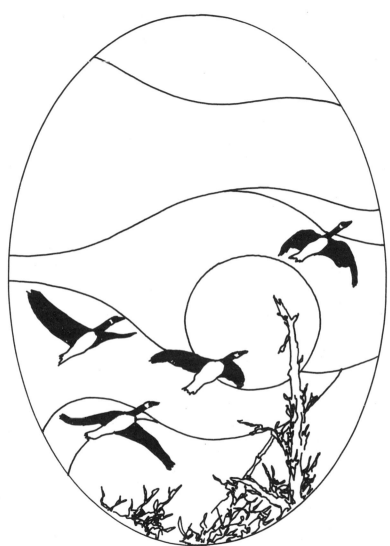

For everything there is a season,
and a time for every matter under heaven.
                    —*Ecclesiastes 3:1 RSV*

Make it a rule never to regret and never to look back. Regret is an appalling waste of energy.

—*Katherine Mansfield*

Teach me to live! 'Tis easier far to die—
Gently and silently to pass away—
On earth's long night to close the heavy eye,
And waken in the glorious realms of day.

Teach me that harder lesson—how to live
To serve Thee in the darkest paths of life.
Arm me for conflict, now fresh vigor give,
And make me more than conqu'ror in the strife.
—*Author unknown*

Wish not so much to live long, as to live well.

—*Benjamin Franklin*

Dear Father, the years are spinning by too fast, and I would not choose to have the birthdays come so quickly and relentlessly—for each one takes me farther from the springtime toward the winter. But I thank thee for the love expressed in the little gifts and surprises of this day and pray that with each passing year I may find new opportunities to use my experience of living in sympathetic sharing of the joys and sorrows of others. I thank thee for the loving memory of other birthdays and pray that till the end of my life I may keep an eager, forward-looking spirit. Amen.

—*Josephine Robertson*
"Prayer on an Unwelcome Birthday"

The Gift of Life

If someone says to us, "Why, you don't look your age at all!" we're complimented. Why? If a person, upon hearing that you're forty-five, says, "That's exactly the age I thought you were," we're insulted. Why?

What is the matter with us that we put such a premium on youth? We spend thousands of foolish dollars on cosmetics and hair dyes and operations to look younger than we are, and we're reluctant to admit that we're only buying hope.

Our society just barely manages to tolerate its elderly. It expects them to step aside, get out of the picture, and let the young people take over. And so every older person experiences a sense of loss. They feel they have lost their worth to society; no one needs them any longer. They've done their jobs, raised their children, and now it will be appreciated if they'll step out of the picture. And many elderly people do exactly that. They sit in a corner and talk about the good old days, refusing to acknowledge the time that is upon them. Or they retreat into silent, private worlds of their own and wait to die.

What's going on here? Is this a Christian reaction? Life is to be celebrated, and a Christian can certainly celebrate the accumulated years with thanksgiving. The life cycle, in all its fullness, has been ordained by God, and we have no right to reject or try to ignore any part of it.

Certainly we're not going to be still walking around at eighty years of age with pacifiers in our mouths. We've long ago put away the things of a child. And so there is no sense in clinging to the things of our youth when we are old.

It's good to stop and look back over our lives. Add up the blessings, in all their disguises, which God has given you. God has been working in our lives since our birth and we can look back over the years and see how good he has been to us.

Older people have a lot to offer. If they are the ones who celebrate life, they are the ones who have something to contribute. They have a maturity and knowledge that youth knows nothing about. They are the ones who thank God for the gift of life.

All of us Christians, regardless of our ages, can start now getting ready to celebrate that part of life that comes to us in our later years. Ask God for guidance, ask him to keep the love and laughter in your soul. Ask him to use you for a new, different purpose later on. And praise him for the gift of life—then and now and later on.

God, I'm grateful for life. Help me to see that every single stage of it is good and has its own rewards. Don't let me despise any part or stage of it; help me search for the good in it and enjoy it. It's your great gift to me, and I thank you.   Amen.